Take the Challenge!

Crazy challenges and silly thrills to explore your talents and everyday skills

by
Apryl Lundsten

★ American Girl®

Published by American Girl Publishing, Inc.
Copyright © 2012 by American Girl, LLC

All rights reserved. No part of this book may be used or reproduced in any manner
whatsoever without written permission except in the case of brief quotations
embodied in critical articles and reviews.

Questions or comments? Call 1-800-845-0005,
visit **americangirl.com**, or write to Customer Service,
American Girl, 8400 Fairway Place, Middleton, WI 53562-0497.

Printed in China
12 13 14 15 16 17 18 19 LEO 10 9 8 7 6 5 4 3 2 1

All American Girl marks are trademarks of American Girl, LLC.

Editorial Development: Trula Magruder

Art Direction & Design: Lisa Wilber

Production: Jeannette Bailey, Sarah Boecher, Tami Kepler, Judith Lary

Illustrations: Galia Bernstein

Photography: Kristin Kurt

If a project seems too difficult or when you see this hand,
always ask an adult to help you.

Dear Reader,

Do you love the pulse-racing joy of competing with friends and family in challenges and games? Someone shouts "Go!" and your heart beats a little faster, your breathing speeds up, and your hands start to sweat. Or do you make your best score by yourself, feeling a small thrill as you listen to the clock tick and tock, while trying to top your previous score?

Whether you like to take on challenges alone or try them with friends—or both!—you'll find hours and hours of entertainment inside. Challenge yourself on rainy days and holidays, times alone and times with crowds. Challenge yourself and your friends for one minute or for an entire weekend.

People have always played games and challenged themselves. Why? Because games help teach us to believe in ourselves. They show us that we have the potential to succeed—whether it's for one minute or for a lifetime. So, "Go!"

Your friends at American Girl

Task Blasters

Everyday tasks can become motivational challenges. Turn homework, team improvements, and simple goals into feverish fun simply by saying "Go!"

Let's say you need to clean your room, but it feels like an enormous chore. Divide this big job into smaller tasks—**taking it one step at a time.**

- Make my bed.
- Put away my things.
- Dust the dresser.
- Clean the mirror.
- Vacuum the carpet.

Now give each of these smaller tasks a time limit, a skill level to compete against, or rules to follow. Look at these examples:

- Compete with your sister to see who can make her bed the quickest or the best. Make an award for the winner.

- Turn vacuuming into a game. Make it a rule that once you've vacuumed an area, you can't touch that spot again with your feet. Figure out how to get out of the room!

- Gather a group of friends to travel from your bedroom to theirs, helping clean each other's spaces in a dirty-room dash.

Challenges **motivate you,** help you stay sharp, and offer immediate rewards. Try the challenges in this book. And then tailor the games to **suit your own challenges,** whether they include getting an A on a reading test, improving your flips in gymnastics, or meeting the new girl in school.

Ask First

Have a parent or other adult approve all challenges, crafts, supplies, and your play area before starting. Then make sure your challenge area is clear of all obstacles.

Reward Yourself

For many of these challenges, reward your competitors—or yourself—with a fun mini certificate. Tear each certificate from the back of the book!

Play in Pencil

Work in pencil to score yourself. Then you can improve your score or challenge other people again and again.

About Our Testers

The times or scores from our American Girl (AG) Challenge Crew, girls ages 8 to 10, will give you a reference to compete against when trying the challenges. You'll always see our testers' *average* score or time. This means that we've totaled the results of *all* our testers and divided that total by the number of girls competing.

Scoring Yourself

 This symbol means the challenge is timed. You'll need a stopwatch, a watch with a second hand, or someone to time you.

FUN FOR ONE

Challenge yourself with these timed tasks,
cool crafts, and brain-building games on rainy days,
afternoons alone, or when you're simply stuck waiting.

Dream-Team Gymnast

This balance feat needs your focus.
Stand on one foot any way you like.
Now shut your eyes, and focus on
your breathing—inhaling and exhaling
slowly. On "Go!" try to keep your foot
off the floor for 1 minute. About 62
percent of the AG Challenge Crew
kept their balance.

☐ **I have a gymnast's balance.**

Balance Beam 🕐

To improve your balance, try this
challenge. Imagine you're a gymnast on
a balance beam. Stand on one foot while
holding your other foot in the hand
nearest that foot. Extend your other
arm to help you adjust your balance.
On "Go!" you have 1 minute to hold this
pose. A full 100 percent of the AG
Challenge Crew perfected this pose.

☐ **I balance like a famous gymnast.**

Moon Dance ⏱

Blow up and tie off **two round yellow balloons**. On "Go!" you must keep both balloons in the air for 1 minute. Only 37 percent of the AG Challenge Crew mastered this task.

☐ **I'm a true moon dancer.**

Hot Potato ⏱

Using any body part except your hands, keep a **balloon** in the air for 1 minute. Tap the "hot potato" with your head, arms, knees, or feet to keep it from touching the ground. About 62 percent of the AG Challenge Crew floated this challenge.

☐ **My spud stayed in the air.**

Diamond Ring ⏱

Love this game, or love it not? Give it a try to see! On "Go!" balance a **white balloon** on the top of your hand for 1 minute. About 87 percent of the AG Challenge Crew sported their diamonds for the full minute.

☐ **My ring was a sure thing.**

Flying Carpets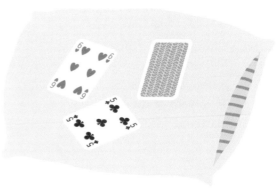

Place a **white pillow** on your bed 3 feet in front of you, and hold a **deck of cards**. On "Go!" you have 1 minute to send one card at a time soaring to the pillow. The AG Challenge Crew landed 8 "flying carpets" on their "cloud."

My soaring score: _____

Headwind

Go ahead and blow this task! Turn a **heavy drinking glass** upside down on a **table**, and place a **deck of cards** on top of the glass. In ONE breath, try to blow off as many cards as you can. The AG Challenge Crew blew off 31 cards.

I "blew" this score: _____

Bean Counter

Fill a **clear plastic bag or jar** with **jelly beans.** Now estimate how many beans are in the container, and write down that number below. Next, count the actual number of jelly beans, and jot down that number. How close were you? The AG Challenge Crew guesses were only 14 beans off!

My guess: _____

My container held _____

My difference was _____

Candy Sucker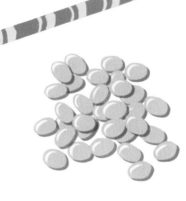

Don't blow this task! Pile **large-sized jelly beans** onto a **clean surface.** On "Go!" suck a jelly bean against a **drinking straw,** and then move it to a sorting pile. See how many beans you can sort into same-colored piles in 1 minute. The AG Challenge Crew sorted 12 candies.

My sorting score: _____

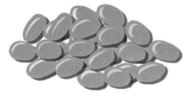

Toe Truck

Keep on your toes to win this task. Stack a **pile of socks** next to an **empty bucket, basket,** or **box.** On "Go!" pick up socks from the pile with your toes and place them in the bucket. You have 1 minute to pick up as many socks as you can. The AG Challenge Crew bucketed 22 socks.

My top toe score: _____

Big Foot

You shouldn't get cold feet trying this challenge! Gather **a collection of socks in various sizes and styles.** Put a sock over each arm so that your hands are covered. On "Go!" see how many socks you can slip on a foot in 1 minute. **Tip:** Start with the thinnest socks first. The AG Challenge Crew slipped on 11 socks.

My sock score: _____

Money Tree

You'll need **15 cups** and a **collection of pennies** for this challenge. Arrange the cups as shown below. Place a piece of **masking tape** on the floor 3 feet from the cups. Stand behind the tape, making sure not to lean over it. You have 1 minute to try to toss a penny into each cup. The AG Challenge Crew landed pennies in 7 cups.

My penny-to-cup score: _____

How to make a playing-card building block

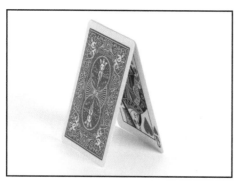

1. Lean two **playing cards** together so that they stand like a tent.
Tip: Tape the cards together at the top if they're too new to stand.

2. Create another tent next to the first.

3. Center a card over the two points. This is your building block. Balance another tent on top.

4. Add another tent on the bottom and you can build 3 stories high. Add a fourth, and you can build 4 stories high, and so on.

Housework

This challenge will floor you! Starting with a **deck of playing cards,** see how many cards you can use to erect a house. Try to complete as many stories as you can before your building collapses.

My floor score: _____

My total card score: _____

Canal Cruiser

To float this boat, build a canal. Place **masking tape** on **cardboard** or a crafting table in two 3-foot-long rows that are about 5 inches apart. Make a **gondola** (see the instructions to make one on the right-hand page), and then place the boat at the canal entry. Use a **drinking straw** to blow your boat from one end of the canal to the other. If you blow more than half of your boat across the tape, you must start over, so blow cautiously. All 100 percent of the AG Challenge Crew cruised their gondolas through the canals.

☐ **I sailed through this task.**

Grand Gondola

Fold a boat that will float through a challenge! To make it, remove one sheet of the origami paper from the back of this book, and follow these instructions.

1. Fold the **origami paper** into a long rectangle. Crease sharply.

2. Open the paper, and fold in each long side so that it touches the center crease.

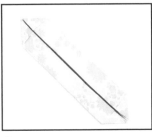

3. Fold each corner into a small triangle that nearly touches the center crease.

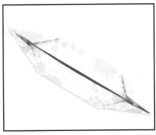

4. Fold each triangle toward the center crease again, making a slightly longer triangle.

5. Open the center flaps, and *carefully* turn the boat inside out. Hold the triangles closed as you flip the ends.

6. Press out any creases.

Name-Calling

These names are as pretty as a picture! For this challenge, you have 1 minute to use the picture and letter combinations below to decipher girls' names. It may help to say these out loud. Check your answers in the back of this book.

1. [apple core] + T + [boot]

2. [bell] + A

3. [seal] + OR

4. [arch] + IT

5. [shell] + [bee]

6. [pebbles] + AN

7. [eye] + [girl]

8. [stick/wand] + A

My smart score: _____

Block Buster

You have 1 minute to solve these puzzles! Figure out the compound word or short phrase in each box. Check your answers in the back of this book.

1. feeling

2. Dutch Dutch

3. tree

4. tickled

5. fish

6. pig pig pig

7. Jack

8. berries

9. dare dare

10. thumb

11. ↓ strike strike strike you

12. FA RED CE

My block-buster score: _____

Zookeeper

Draw these animals out of hiding. To complete the challenge, rearrange the letters in each word below to find an animal. For example, "wee" would become "ewe." You have 1 minute to find as many animals as you can. If you get stuck, move on to a different word. Check your answers in the back of this book.

1. pea   _____

2. calm   _____

3. tab   _____

4. hear   _____

5. paws   _____

6. reed   _____

7. act   _____

8. flow   _____

9. tan   _____

10. shore   _____

11. low   _____

12. balm   _____

13. lee   _____

14. went   _____

15. god   _____

16. sale   _____

17. tar   _____

18. gun   _____

19. bare   _____

20. tang   _____

My wild score: _____

Super Girl ⏱

Build up your strength for gymnastics or other sports with this core-building move. Lie on your stomach on a **mat** or **carpet.** On "Go!" lift your head, arms, legs, and chest off the ground. You have 1 minute to "fly" without touching the floor. About 87 percent of the AG Challenge Crew soared for 1 minute.

☐ **I flew through this task.**

Core Score ⏱

All of our movements are made using our torso, or core. Strengthening this area improves our bodies for sports or everyday mobility. Try this core challenge. Lie on your back on a **mat** or **carpet.** On "Go!" lift your legs straight off the ground, reach your arms in the air toward your legs, and hold the pose for 1 minute. About 62 percent of the AG Challenge Crew mastered this task.

☐ **I have a powerful core.**

Fly Catcher

Lie on the floor on your back. On "Go!" you have 1 minute to toss a **tennis ball** into the air and catch it as many times as you can. Once you drop the ball, stop counting.

Tougher: Try again, but this time clap between throws. The AG Challenge Crew caught 30 fly balls.

My catching score: _____

Dribble Drill

Follow the bouncing ball! Stand with your feet shoulder-width apart. Dribble a **tennis ball** as many times as you can in 1 minute. Count out loud to help keep track. The AG Challenge Crew dribbled the ball 88 times!

My dribbling score: _____

Goofy Golf

Place **3 large paper cups** on their sides and set them about 6 steps apart within an **open area,** such as a patio or hallway. Tape the cups in place. Take 6 steps back, and using your toe as a golf club, carefully tap a **tennis ball** into a cup, keeping track of the number of "strokes" you take to get into that "hole." Remove the ball from that cup, and then tap it into the next one. Total the number of strokes (taps) for all 3 holes. The AG Challenge Crew played a round in 13 strokes.

My putting score: _____

Bitty Bowling

Strike out to win this game! Stand **10 clothespins** at the end of an **open area** or **hallway** in a triangular placement with rows of 4, 3, 2, and 1. Place the clothespins about 1½ inches apart. Take 5 giant steps back, and roll a **tennis ball.** You get 2 rolls to knock down as many pins as you can. The AG Challenge Crew knocked down about 6 pins.

My bowling score: _____

State Line

Using the **book's US map**, you have 1 minute to draw a line through each of the 48 continental states—without ever crossing your line twice! About 62 percent of the AG Challenge Crew went through each state without backtracking over their lines.

My traveling count: _____

See the States

Study the names of the states on the **book's US map** for 30 seconds. Then flip the map over to write on it. On "Go!" you have 1 minute to name as many states as you can remember. Stumped? Think about states that friends and family live in, places you've seen on TV, or vacation spots you'd like to visit. The AG Challenge Crew guessed 17 states.

My state score: _____

Map Mailer

Make the miles apart the focus of a special envelope.

⭐ With an adult's help, carefully open a **plain envelope** to use as a pattern, or look for a pattern online. Lay the pattern over an **old map.** If you like, use a map of your hometown or city! Trace the pattern, and cut out the envelope. Fold the map, following your envelope pattern, and seal it with a **glue stick.** Use the envelope to send a card or letter to faraway family or friends.

All in the Family

How well do you know those closest to you? Try this challenge to find out. First, choose 3 adult family members. Write down their full names (including their middle names). Second, write down where each person was born. Next, write down each person's job. If the person is retired, write down what she or he did before retirement. Finally, write down each person's favorite restaurant. To check your answers, ask each family member these questions. How many answers did you get right?

My family score: _____

Topeka ★
KANSAS

Name: _____

Birthplace: _____

Job: _____

Favorite restaurant: _____

Name: _____

Birthplace: _____

Job: _____

Favorite restaurant: _____

Name: _____

Birthplace: _____

Job: _____

Favorite restaurant: _____

Copper Topper

Start at the bottom to accomplish this challenge. Carefully drop one penny on top of another. Don't straighten the stack as you go! Pile the coins until your stack topples. Then total the number of pennies you used. The AG Challenge Crew stacked 21 pennies.

My penny-stack total: _____

TESTS FOR TWO

Try these challenges with a friend, sibling, parent, or other play partner. For even more fun, record wins in pencil so that you can challenge your buddy again!

Penny Pile

How well will you stack up against your opponent? While blindfolded, stack a collection of pennies one at a time to create a penny pile. You can touch the pile to figure out where to place your coin, but if you accidentally knock over the pile, you're done. After your pile falls, record the number of pennies, and then pass the blindfold to your partner.

My stack score: _____

My partner's stack score: _____

Bank Teller

This time you'll create your opponent's stack and she'll create yours. One of you wears a blindfold and listens very carefully to the other's directions about where to place a collection of pennies one at a time. This time, you cannot feel the stack. When the stack falls, record the number of pennies, and then switch places.

My stack score: _____

My partner's stack score: _____

Did You Know?
Abe Lincoln is on both sides of a penny. Take a magnifying glass and look closely between the pillars inside the monument on the back of a new penny. See the tiny Abe?

Cave In

Wet a facial tissue, place it over a paper cup, and hold it tightly in place around the cup's rim with a rubber band. Gather a collection of pennies. You and your opponent take turns gently adding a penny to the tissue until it collapses from the weight. The one to collapse the tissue loses.

Tight Race

A good penny pincher will win this game! Spread out 20 pennies on a table. You and your opponent each take one side of the same clean pair of old nylons or tights (ask a parent first!) and work your hand to the toe. On "Go! the first to pick up 10 pennies and place them in her pile wins.

The Penny Pincher award goes to

_____

Just for Fun

It costs only 1 cent to make a wish, so toss a penny into a park fountain and make yours.

Pencil Plunge

Take the time to let this task sink in. Loosely tie a string around your arm. Then tie the end of the string to a pencil so that the pencil dangles about 1 foot from your elbow. Place an empty plastic soda or water bottle on the ground in front of you. Hold the pencil in your hand, and on "Go!" see how quickly you can sink it into the bottle. You can't touch the pencil or string. Now let your partner test her sinking skills.

My plunging-pencil time: _____

My partner's plunging-pencil time: _____

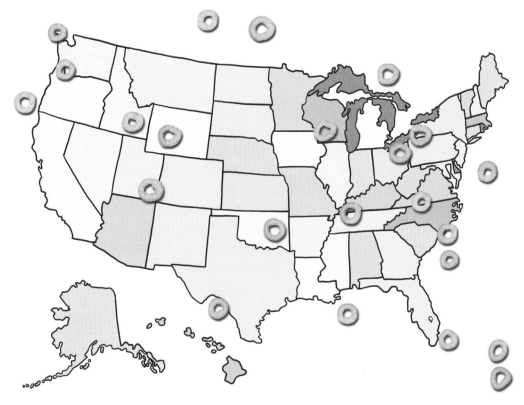

O, America!

Place the US map from the back of this book on the floor—you may need to place small objects on the corners to hold it flat. Stand on opposite sides of the map. Give your opponent one color of O-shaped cereal and you take another color. On "Go!" you and your opponent take turns holding an arm straight over the map and dropping a cereal O completely within each border of the 6 largest US states listed below. The first to land on all of the 6 states wins.

- Alaska
- Texas
- California
- Montana
- New Mexico
- Arizona

The State Champion award goes to _____

Book Delivery

This challenge is by the book! You and an opponent take turns choosing 5 lightweight books each and placing your stack on one side of a room. On "Go!" you each balance a book on your head and deliver it to the opposite side of the room. Note: Once the book is balanced, you can't touch it again. If the book falls or if you touch it before you've reached your destination, you must go back to your book pile and rebalance the book. The first to get all her books to the opposite side wins.

The Book It award goes to

_____

Magazine Rack

Pile stacks of magazines on opposite sides of a room. On "Go!" you and an opponent place a single magazine on your head, cross the room, bend down and add another magazine to your head, return, add another, and so on until all your magazines fall off. You can't straighten the stack, but you can open the magazine to spread it over your head. Who added the most magazines to her head rack?

The Zine Queen award goes to

_____

Picnic Basket

You and your opponent each place a paper plate, paper cup, paper napkin, and plastic spoon on your head in any way you'd like to balance them. You can't touch the pieces again once they're settled on your head. On "Go!" the one who can walk the farthest before all of her picnic slips off wins!

The Picnic Packer award goes to

_____

Haiku View

A haiku is a form of Japanese poetry with 3 lines. The first line has 5 syllables, the second line has 7 syllables, and the third line has 5 syllables. For this poetic challenge, you have 1 minute to create a haiku for each of the topics shown at right. If you both finish the poems, ask an impartial judge to choose the one that best fits each topic. The best 2 out of 3 wins.

The Haiku Know-How award goes to

_____

- A friend
- A sport or hobby
- Something in nature

Hidden Haiku

Do you and your opponent have the poetic power to uncover a hidden haiku? To find out, both of you will need an **old magazine, scissors, glue,** and **extra paper.** First, ask a parent if you can cut out pages from the magazine. Next, each of you chooses your own topic from the list at left. Finally, search through your magazine, cut out words to write your haiku, and glue them in the 5-7-5 syllable order on your page. Again, ask an impartial judge to pick the one that best suits the topic you've each selected.

The Poetic Pluck award goes to

- A season
- An animal
- A place

_____

Baby Talk

Help your friendship grow by discovering 5 new things about each other as babies. Read the questions below, and write down your guesses about your friend while she writes down her guesses about you. Now, switch papers to see how many you each got correct. If either of you can't answer a question about yourself, take it to a parent to check!

What was your friend's first word?

Who was her favorite relative?

Why did her parents choose her name?

What was her favorite toy?

In what state was she born?

Grasshoppers

Hop to this challenge! Find a grassy area that's clear of rocks or other obstacles, and ask a parent if you can use 2 old pillowcases. You and an opponent each climb inside a pillowcase. Choose a landing spot in the yard, such as a tree or the edge of a driveway. On "Go!" be the first to hop to that spot.

The Top Hopper award goes to

_____

Best Buds

You and your friend sit on the floor back-to-back with arms linked. On "Go!" you have 1 minute to stand up on one leg without falling over. To help keep your balance, make sure one of you uses her left leg to stand up while the other uses her right leg.

We grew as friends in _____ seconds.

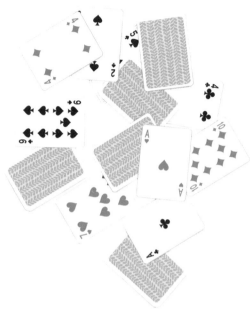

Messy Matches

Play your cards right to win this challenge. Spread an entire deck of playing cards facedown over the floor in a random, messy manner. You and a friend take turns flipping over two cards each. If the cards match, you keep the set. (A match is two cards with the same number but not necessarily the same color.) If they don't, flip the cards back over. When all the cards have been picked up, each of you counts your cards to see who has the most pairs.

The Marvelous Memory award goes to

_____

Grab Bag 🕑

Taking turns, go into a room, find 10 small objects, and slip them into a paper bag. On "Go!" dump the objects in front of your opponent, and after 30 seconds, return them to the bag. Your opponent must wait for 30 seconds and then try to list all the objects in the bag. Next, switch roles, with your opponent finding all new objects.

The Mind Magician award goes to

_____

Crazy Eights

Look after number 1 in this challenge. Take turns counting by 8s aloud. You say 8, your friend says 16, you say 24, and so on. See how high you can count without pauses. If you pause for more than a second or two, you're out! Try again with a different number.

The Great Eights award goes to

_____

Two to Tango

Don't dance around this task. On "Go!" begin at number 1 and take turns alternating the count as quickly as you can. However, anytime you arrive at a number with a "2," such as 12, 20 through 29, and so on, you must say "tango" instead.

Tougher: Try this with an additional number so that you have to identify two "tango" numbers at the same time!

The Tango Trotter award goes to

_____

TANGO!

Digit Decoder

You and an opponent each secretly write down 5 sets of numerals between 1 and 6. You can repeat as many numbers as you like. Say you've written these numbers on your paper:

2 6　　2 6　　1 1　　4 3　　5 4

Now your opponent rolls a **pair of dice**. If she rolls a 2 and a 6, she can cross that set off your paper. If she rolls a 2 and a 4, she can't. The first one to roll all the sets written on her opponent's sheet wins.

The Golden Roller award goes to

_____

Roll Bowl

Take turns rolling the **dice**. Cross off the number on the pin that matches the total score on the dice. Let's say you roll a 4 and a 4. You'd cross off the 8 pin. If you roll a number that's already been crossed off, just pass the dice to your opponent. The one to cross off the final pin wins!

The Pinsetter award goes to

_____

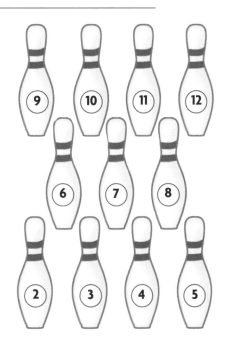

Sweet Service

Challenge yourself and a partner to perform 20 acts of kindness in 1 month. During a chosen month, you and a parent, sibling, or friend (working as a pair or alone) will perform the acts of kindness (see below, plus add your own ideas).

☐ Offer to help study with a classmate who's struggling with her homework.

☐ Make friends with someone who's new to your team or school.

☐ Take the time to read books to your younger siblings.

☐ Make a card for a favorite teacher or a great substitute teacher.

☐ Write a thank-you note to a parent or grandparent who goes out of his or her way to help you.

☐ Hold open the door for someone who needs extra help.

☐ Hold open the door for someone older.

☐ With a parent's help, drop off books and magazines at the children's ward of a hospital.

☐ With a parent's help, take clothing or blankets to a shelter for homeless people.

☐ With a parent's help, make treats for someone who's sad.

☐ Set the table without being asked.

☐ Send a card to a faraway relative just to say hi.

☐ Tell a friend one thing you love about her.

☐ Donate your pocket change to a charity box on a store counter.

☐ Create a "School's Cool" poster. Ask your teacher if you can hang it up.

☐ Make a cute craft that's appropriate for a younger child, and then surprise your sibling or a friend's sibling with the craft.

☐ _____

☐ _____

☐ _____

☐ _____

Our kindness count: _____

Money Box

Gather a collection of change, and slip 10 coins into a tissue box. On "Go!" your opponent has 1 minute to count the total amount of money in the box by slipping her hand in the hole and feeling the coins. After time is up, dump the box to check. Then switch with a new set of coins.

The Bank Teller award goes to

_____

Puzzle Box

One of you takes the front of a cereal box and one of you takes the back. Use scissors to cut the cardboard into puzzle pieces. Get creative with your shapes. On "Go!" trade puzzles and see who can complete her side of the cereal box the fastest!

The Puzzle Assembler award goes to

_____

Tic-Tac-Throw

Line up 9 clear plastic cups in 3 rows so that the glasses are all touching. You and your opponent each take 3 giant steps back from your own side of the glasses and mark the spot on the floor with masking tape. Each chooses a different color of pom-poms. On "Go!" take turns tossing a pom-pom into any glass. The first player to get 3 pom-poms in a line in any direction wins.

Tougher: If one player's pom-pom lands on top of another player's pom-pom, that space can't be used by either player.

The Terrific Tosser award goes to

_____

Pom-Pom Platter

Place 6 paper plates on top of 6 paper cups, and line them up in a row. You and your opponent each take 2 giant steps back from your own side of the plates and mark the spot on the floor with masking tape. Each chooses a different color of pom-poms. On "Go!" the first player to get one of her colored pom-poms on each plate wins.

The Platter Pride award goes to

_____

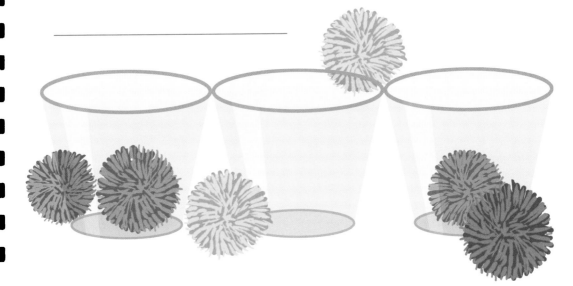

Back Track

You and a friend sit back-to-back. Choose one person whom you both know well, such as a classmate or teacher. Each of you lists 5 things that describe that person, such as "smart" or "movie lover." No peeking! Now compare your lists. Did any descriptions match? Record your results below.

Our shared score: _____

Best Buds

This time write down 5 things that you think describe each other. Did any match? Without discussion, repeat the challenge until all 5 descriptions match on both of your lists. But remember: you can't discuss which words you'll each choose.

Kindness Counts

When you think a parent is under a lot of stress, surprise her or him by helping out with a chore. Help before your parent asks you to do it or before she or he does the chore.

Craft Challenge

Bookmark Bonding

Keep a bookmark close that you and a best friend color together. You and a friend will use colored pencils or markers to color one side of a bookmark from the back of the book. Then switch bookmarks and color the opposite side. After you've finished, each take a bookmark. When using the bookmark, flip it from your side to your friend's to remind yourself of the time you colored together.

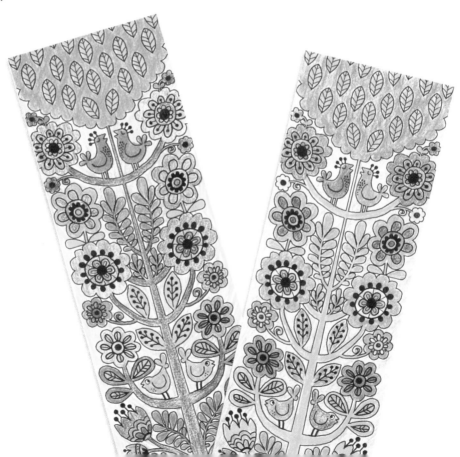

Distant Decision

Give an opponent a ball of yarn and keep
one for yourself. Point out an object across
the room or yard, such as a chair or a basketball.
Using scissors, each of you cuts a piece of
yarn to the size that you think will fit perfectly
around that object. Now measure. The one
closest to being correct keeps both
pieces of yarn. Now try another object.
The player with the most yarn after 5 tries wins.

The Size Wise award goes to

_____

Identical Twins

Separate 5 pairs of socks, slip them
inside a pillowcase, and mix them up.
On "Go!" you have 1 minute to correctly
mate all the socks without looking.
Drop the bag when you're done or if
time runs out. Check your mates, and
count the sock pairs correctly mated.
Now switch players.

The Great Mate award goes to

_____

Detective Dig ⏱

Fill a brown paper bag with various objects from the house or yard. Your opponent sticks her hand into the bag and writes down as many objects as she can identify in 1 minute. The player who guesses the most wins.

The Soft Touch award goes to _____

Revise and Visualize

This challenge will help you to focus on the facts when you're reading homework, a chapter book, or any other writing. Read one of the sentences below with a friend. Before reading the next one, each of you must describe in detail the words in that sentence popped in color. For example, if the word bike was popped, you might say, "It's a blue bike with a horn, basket, and red, white, and blue steamers." Your friend might say, "It's a red ten-speed with racing stripes." Then move on to the next one. Are your descriptions alike or *very* different?

Even though she was young, Janice excelled at baking. Her pastries were prized by all her classmates. She loved baking cupcakes and cookies. She even had her own apron! Sometimes, she invented desserts, such as her Cake-In-a-Cone or her Fruity Float. Everyone loved being invited to her parties, because they knew their stomachs would be doing the celebrating.

GAMES
FOR GROUPS

At sleepovers, during school recess, at parties, or when you're visiting cousins—challenge your group get-togethers with games, tasks, crafts, and quizzes!

Copycats

Ask a nonplayer to write down a list of nouns. She'll need 3 nouns for 6 players, 4 nouns for 8 players, and so on. Copy the list, and use **scissors** to cut each set of words into strips. Mix up the strips in a **bowl,** and ask each player to pick one. On "Go!" each player pantomimes her word. When a player finds the other player acting out the same noun, the two stand side by side and shout their noun out loud in unison. If they're the first pair to make a match, they win 1 point each. Repeat the game with all-new nouns. The first player to earn 3 points wins.

The Double Trouble award goes to _____

Match Mate 🕑

Meet your match in this challenge. Put a collection of **different matching objects** in a **large bowl**. It can include anything and everything—erasers, balls, buttons, beads—as long as there are at least two of each object that match. Pour the objects onto the **floor** or a **table.** On "Go!" players around the table have 1 minute to scramble and find the most matches. Watch out! Someone may be holding the same object you're trying to match.

The Batches of Matches award goes to _____

Family Business

Try this task with the family. Working together, brainstorm a business idea. Make up something outlandish, or create an idea that actually could work. Come up with both types of ideas, just to see what might spark. Now market your products —make posters, write a catchy jingle, or videotape a silly TV ad.

Our family business name:

What our business does:

_____   _____

Grocery List

For this challenge, you'll need to talk shop. Gather **10 pantry items,** such as cereal or pasta. Players try to guess the price of each item. (To find prices, ask a parent to help you check receipts, look online, or take you to the market.) Players get a point for each item they get closest to the price. The player with the most points wins!

The Smart Shopper award goes to

_____

Royal Recall

Pull out the face cards and aces from a **deck of cards,** and shuffle the rest of the cards. Deal an even number of cards to each player. One at a time, each player guesses which card is on top of her pile. She then holds the card up to the other players, but she can't see it herself. The players say yes or no, depending on whether or not the guesser is right. If she's wrong, the player slips the card back on top of her pile, and the next player tries. If she's right, she gets to remove the card from her pile. The first player to guess all her cards correctly wins the game.

The Card Sharp award goes to _____

Craft Club

Gather your friends and challenge them to make a special craft. Choose one of the craft challenges listed below. Take a few days to make the craft, and then come together to share your creations. Or, if you like, gather supplies and make the crafts as a group at a sleepover or another special occasion. For even more fun, give the team a tight timeline for completing the task.

- ☐ Design a bookmark based on a popular book.

- ☐ Create a scrapbook page about a sleepover.

- ☐ Decorate a cupcake that looks like your favorite animal.

- ☐ Make a wall craft using your initials.

- ☐ Accent a frame for a parent.

- ☐ Transform a piece of old clothing into something new.

- ☐ Use buttons to update an old pillow.

- ☐ Create fancy table place cards for a special meal.

- ☐ Design a card for your teacher relating to the next holiday.

- ☐ Transform a candy tin into something special.

Dot Art

Set out various colors of **nontoxic paint**. Give each person a sheet of **drawing paper** and **5 cotton swabs**. Choose something in the room, such as a bowl of fruit or a cat sleeping on a chair. Or pick an item from memory, such as a flower or an animal. Once you've all agreed on the subject, each person must **paint** it using the cotton swabs—but use only dots to create the image.

Dashing Dresser

Clothes make the woman in this game! Give each player a **clean trash bag** containing a **pair of gloves**, a **large pair of pants**, a **T-shirt**, a **pair of socks**, a **scarf**, and a **hat**. On "Go!" players must get dressed as quickly as they can. Whoever dons every item first wins.

Tougher: Choose a partner and be the first pair to swap outfits with each other!

The Quick Change award goes to

_____

Slashin' Fashion

Turn a drab tee into fab fashion! On "Go!" each player, using her own **scissors** and her own **old T-shirt** (ask a parent first), must transform the shirt into something new. Once everyone is finished, slip the shirts on and hold a fashion show. **Tips:** Cut off the neckband to change the neckline. Cut the bottom of the shirt into a strip to use for a belt. Slit the sides of the tee to give it a new shape. Cut fringe along the bottom. Cut straight and angled rectangles across the front so that your own shirt shows through.

Daisy Dash 🕐

Place **2 pads of paper**, **2 pencils**, and **2 empty flower pots** in the center of a **table**. Divide into 2 teams and stand across the room from the table. Decide who will go first, second, third, and so on. On "Go!" the first player from each team runs to the table, writes down any letter from the word "DAISY," folds the paper, and tosses it into her team's pot. She then runs back to tag the next player. After 5 minutes, each team unfolds its slips of paper and sees how many D-A-I-S-Ys can be made. The team that gathers the most wins.

The Flower Power award goes to _____

Chicken Run

You'll need **2 boxes** and a **clear, open area** for this game. Place a box (the coop) at each end of the playing area. Position players (the chickens) at each box. On "Go!" players squat down with their hands held under their armpits like chickens and dash across the yard to the opposite coop. The first player to touch the opposite coop wins the round. Play 5 rounds. Whoever wins the most rounds is the champion.

The Champion Chicken award goes to

_____

Lame Duck

Choose a player to be the Hunter. The Hunter must tag each player (a duck) 4 times—on each wing (arm) and each leg. When the Hunter tags a player, the limb she tagged can't bend. Once someone gets all four limbs tagged, she's out. The last duck in wins.

The Lucky Duck award goes to

_____

Reporter's Notebook

Give each player **paper**, a **pen**, and a **news story** from a newspaper. Each player writes Who, What, Where, When, and Why on her paper, and then studies her story. On "Go!" players write down who's the star of the story, what the story is about, where it takes place, when it takes place, and why the story is news. The first person to write each of these for her story is the chief reporter.

The Rad Reporter award goes to

_____

Silly Stories

Here's the scoop. Each person uses **scissors** to cut out headlines, words, photos, and paragraphs from her own section of a **newspaper**. On "Go!" players use their clips to create their own silly news stories. Or players can team up to create a totally off-the-wall piece.

The Silliest Storyteller award goes to

_____

Balancing Act

Skills like standing on one leg in gymnastics, reaching into the fridge, or slipping on your pants all require amazing balance. Improve your balance by practicing when you can. Try this: Each player stands, wets the inside "bowl" of her own **spoon,** and hangs the spoon on her nose. On "Go!" everyone lifts a foot off the ground while keeping the spoon balanced on her nose. The player who stands the longest without losing her spoon wins.

The Steadiest Spoon award goes to _____

It's Like ...

A word to the wise . . . The first player opens a **dictionary** and randomly reads aloud a word everyone knows, such as "big." The player on her right has 20 seconds to come up with a word that means the same thing (a *synonym*), such as "large" or "giant." If a player can't come up with a word in time or says a wrong word, she's out. Once all players have chosen a synonym, the dictionary rotates. If Player X can't think of a synonym but another person in the group can, Player X is out. If no one can, the dictionary rotates, and the game begins again. The last person remaining wins. **Note:** If a player's synonym is unfamiliar, use the dictionary to look up its meaning.

The Word Wizard award goes to

_____

Star Smarts

Learning to follow the logic of a story can greatly improve reading comprehension. This game helps advance those skills by requiring players to use logic and word clues to quickly fill in sentence gaps. To play, you'll need **paper stars**, a few **books**, and friends. On "Go!" someone reads a sentence from a book but deletes a verb or noun in that sentence and replaces it with the word *star*. As soon as the reader finishes the sentence, the first person to shout out the correct word wins a star. The one with the most stars after everyone reads wins!

The Superstar award goes to

_____

... pet care involves many things including feeding and grooming. It also means petting them and giving them exercise

Suave Improv

Do you have the gift of gab? Each player writes 2 topics on slips of **paper,** such as "pet care" or "playing the piano." Place the slips in a **bowl.** On "Go!" the first player picks a slip from the bowl and starts talking about the topic. The player who can chatter the longest about the topic without stopping, repeating, or going off topic wins.

The Chatting Champion award goes to _____

Toothpick Triangles

See how well you know the angles in this game. Give each person **7 blunt-ended toothpicks.** On "Go!" see who can make 3 triangles the fastest.

The Triangular Ace award goes to

_____

Tower of Treats

This challenge might be fun at a dinner party. Each player must connect **blunt-ended toothpicks** using **marshmallows** or **grapes** as hinges. On "Go!" see who can make the tallest tower the fastest.

The Tallest Tower award goes to

_____

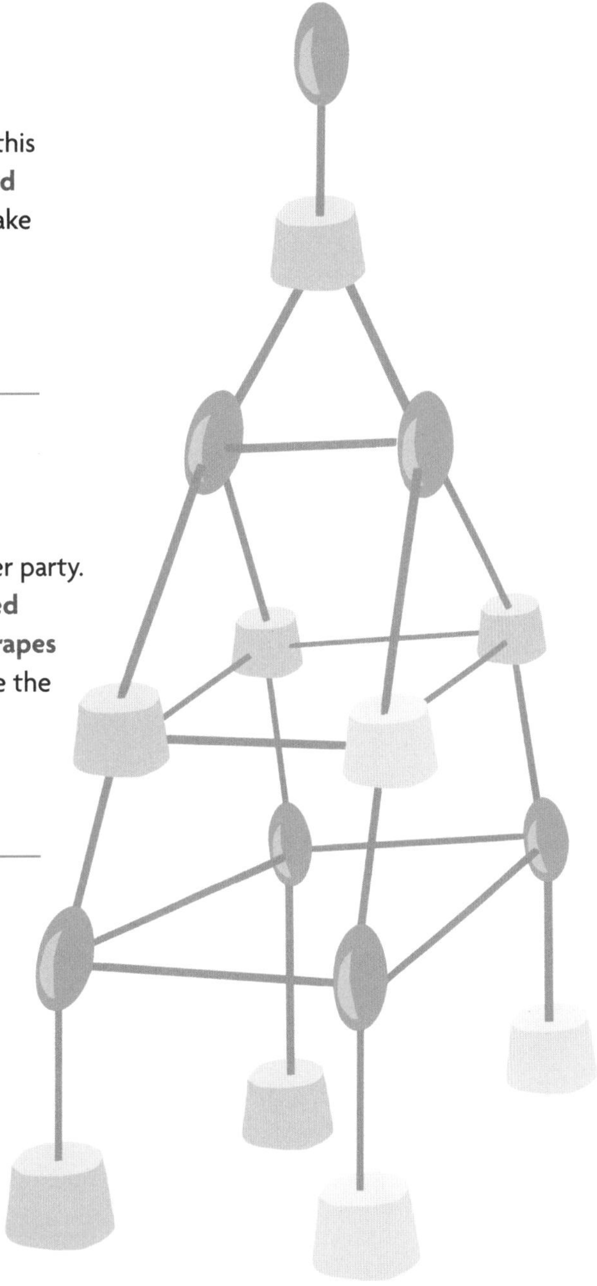

Island Life

Divide into teams. Each team spreads a **blanket** on the ground. All the team members stand on the blanket—their "island." Without getting off the island, each team folds the blanket in toward them, trying to create the smallest island without anyone falling off.

The Tiniest Island award goes to _____

Island Essentials

Give each player a **magazine** and a pair of **scissors**. Have each person secretly cut out 5 items that she thinks would be most useful on a desert island. (Ask an adult before cutting up the magazines.) Slip these inside a **paper bag**. Once everyone's done, mix up the clippings. Now dump out all the items for everyone to see. The entire group can choose only 5 items total. Hold up 1 item at a time and vote on it. Write down the votes for each item. The 5 items with the most votes win. Then give each person who cut out that item a point. The player with the most points wins.

The Ultimate Usability award goes to

_____

Horseshoe Hobby

Make three U-shaped "horseshoes" with **colored or plain craft sticks** (or Popsicle sticks). **Glue** the sticks together where the ends meet. Let dry. Decorate each horseshoe with **stickers or markers** to personalize it. Display the shoes at home or school, or use them for the next game!

Pony Play

Place a **16-ounce bottle filled with water** about 4 feet away from players. You can move the bottle closer or farther away, depending on how hard or easy you want the challenge to be. Each player takes turns throwing her **3 craft-stick horseshoes.** Give 4 points for each shoe that lands on the bottle, 2 points for each shoe that touches the bottle, and 1 point for each shoe that is within 5 inches of the bottle. After 3 rounds, the winner with the most points is champ!

The Head of Horseshoes award goes to

_____

Candy Toss

Place an **egg carton** in the middle of a **table** or **on the floor** at least 3 feet away from players. Each player is then given 10 same-colored candies from a **bag of candies**. The first player tosses a piece of candy into one of the egg cups. The second player does the same, and so on. The object is to get 3 candies of the same color into one cup. The player who lands her third candy in the cup gets 1 point and gets to keep all the candies in that cup. The first player with 3 points wins.

The Three-of-a-Kind award goes to _____

DARING PLAYS FOR HOLIDAYS

Make holidays and winter days even jollier with themed challenges for friends and family.

Frozen Lips

Silence is golden in this game. Divide into 2 teams, and give each team a name. Tell players that thanks to a winter storm, everyone's lips are frozen shut. Now, line up according to height, tallest to shortest. Next, each team lines up in the order of each team member's birthday. (A player born on January 1 would be first in line.) Now, create your own ways to line up. Remember—no talking! For each successful challenge, that team will get a point. The team with the most points wins!

The Strong and Silent award goes to

_____

Cold Foot

On "Go!" you and a friend freeze one foot on the ground and lift the other into the air in a comfortable position. Try placing your lifted foot on your inner leg just above or below your knee. How long can you keep that foot from touching the ground?

The Frozen Foot award goes to

_____

Snowball Fight

Poke your nose into this challenge! Give each player a small bowl and then scatter lots of **cotton balls** (snowballs) around the **table**. Each player dabs a glob of **petroleum jelly** on the tip of her nose and stands next to the table with a **bowl** nearby. On "Go!" each player must use only her nose to gather up as many snowballs as she can and place them in her bowl. The player with the most snowballs wins!

The Snow Shoveler award goes to

_____

Holiday Cheer

Grab a pile of greeting cards. Stack them one by one. See how many you can stack without knocking them over.

My number of cards used: _____

Stuck Together

This challenge requires strong legs! Sit on the floor with a friend, backs together and arms linked. On "Go!" you have 1 minute to stand up by pushing against each other's backs.

We stood in _____ **seconds.**

Weather Alert

This game is fun at big family gatherings! As people arrive at your house, collect **their winter wear,** such as coats, hats, scarves, and boots. Mix up the items and place them around the room or house in different piles. Divide into teams. Throughout the evening, when players hear, "Winter Warning!" each person must search around the house to find all the clothing he or she arrived in and get dressed. The fastest team wins!

The Best Dressed award goes to

_____

Just for Fun

Cut cards into cheery shapes, such as stars, bells, and angels. Punch a hole in the top with a hole punch and thread a string through the shape for a gift tag.

Mouse Gift

How quickly can you wrap a very tiny gift? Try it! You have 1 minute to wrap a **game die** with **holiday paper** and **clear tape.** How did you do? **Tougher:** Try to wrap a pair of dice in 1 minute!

☐ **I wrapped in a flash!**

Elephant Gift 🕐

🖐 Now see how fast you can wrap a big, bulky object, such as a desk chair. Check with Mom and Dad first to make sure it's OK. Use old wrapping paper, newspapers, or even paper bags and clear tape. Time yourself to see how long it takes.

My gift-wrapping time: _____

Holiday Music

Give players paper and pencils and have them write down the names of two holiday songs. Ask each player to tear the song titles into strips, fold them, and place them in a bowl. Each player takes a turn pulling out a strip and singing or saying the lyrics to that song. The winner is the one who gets all or most of the lyrics to her song correct. Ask an adult to check out the lyrics online if no one is certain.

The Sweet Singer award goes to

_____

Gift of Gab

On "Go!" you and an opponent see who can talk the longest without saying "uh" or "um." The first player to use one of those words is out.

The Motor Mouth award goes to

_____

Santa's Sack

Open up presents to play this game! Divide into 2 teams. Write each player's name on a **gift-wrapped box**, and slip it into a **bag** for her team. On "Go!" a player from each team puts on an **oversized pair of gloves**, finds the gift with her name on it, opens it, returns the gloves to the bag, and then passes the bag to the next player. The first team to open all its gifts wins.

The Gift Grab award goes to _____

Did You Know?
The tradition of gift wrapping began in China, where paper was first invented in AD 105.

Turkey Catcher

Play this game throughout Thanksgiving Day. First, count out as many cards from a deck of playing cards as there are players. Make sure there's only one ace in the stack. Shuffle the cards and deal one to each player. The player who gets the ace is the "Turkey Catcher." All other players are "Turkeys." Players keep their cards a secret. The Catcher must collect as many Turkeys as she can without being caught. She catches one by winking at a Turkey without letting the other Turkeys notice. Once a Turkey is "caught," she must wait 5 seconds, and then dramatically fall to the ground. Turkeys still in the game can try to nab the Catcher by calling her out before she winks at them, but if a Turkey wrongly accuses another Turkey, she's out. The player who identifies the Catcher wins. If no one does, the Catcher wins.

The Tom Turkey award goes to _____

Thanksgiving Feast

This challenge is fun to play while the scents of turkey and pie waft through the air. Players sit in a circle. The first player begins by saying what she loves to eat on Thanksgiving. For example, she might say, "At Thanksgiving dinner, I like to eat pumpkin pie." The next player then repeats, "At Thanksgiving dinner, I like to eat pumpkin pie" and adds her favorite dish. This continues around the circle until each player has taken a turn, reciting items in the exact order and adding a new one. If a player makes a mistake, she is out.

The Delicious Dreamer award goes to

_____

Fact or Fiction?

This challenge requires you to serve up some baloney with the turkey! Taking turns around the dinner table, each person tells a story about herself. It can be either a true story or a made-up one. The other diners then have to guess if the story is true or false. The idea is to stump the other players without being called on your bluff. The person who stumps the most people wins.

The Stupendous Stumper award goes to

_____

Happy Holidaze ⏱

Divide into teams of 3. One player sits on a chair with the other 2 players standing on either side of her. On "ho-ho-ho!" each standing player whispers a made-up holiday story in the sitting player's ears—the crazier, the better! After listening to gobbledygook for 30 seconds, the sitting player tries to retell as much of each story as she can. Switch players until each has had a turn in the hot seat. How far from the originals did the stories get?

_____ Very far   _____ Not that far

Secret Stories

Players sit in a circle. The first player leans over to the player on her right and whispers a silly, made-up holiday story in her ear. The second player whispers the story to the player on her right. Continue whispering the story around the circle until everyone has heard it. The last player tells the story. How far from the original did the story get?

_____ Very far   _____ Not that far

Detail Detective

Practicing reading comprehension skills can be as fun as pretending to be a detective who's trying to solve a great case! To solve your first case, read the passage below, and then turn the page and answer 10 questions about it. If you can answer them without turning back to look, you've solved the case! To play again, ask someone to read another paragraph, page, or chapter from a book or magazine, and write 10 questions about that passage. If you can answer all 10 correctly, you've solved the case! Can you do it?

☐ **I cracked this reading case!**

The September sun warmed the sidewalk outside Almost Home Coffee Shop. Bikes filled the bike rack. Customers sipped warm drinks at outdoor tables as a few dogs rested beside their owners. I headed inside and set the brass bells jingling—*ting-ting, ting-ting*. Smells of fresh-baked cookies, scones, and muffins greeted me. The coffee shop was full of customers chatting, reading, or working on laptops.

"Hi, McKenna," said Mom, stepping out from behind the giant churning coffee roaster, her red apron tied over a skirt. Tucking strands of her sandy hair into a bun, she asked, "So, how was your second Tuesday of school?"

Excerpted from *McKenna* by Mary Casanova

Answer Agent

Answer these questions about the paragraphs on the previous page. No peeking!

1. What month was it? _____

2. What was the name of the coffee shop? _____

3. What was in the rack outside the shop? _____

4. What kind of bells rang on entry to the shop? _____

5. Name one of the desserts that McKenna smelled. _____

6. Who did McKenna know at the shop? _____

7. What kind of animal was mentioned in the scene? _____

8. How did McKenna's mother wear her hair? _____

9. What color was the apron mentioned in the scene? _____

10. Name one of the ways people were spending time in the coffee shop.

_____

Now flip back to check your answers. How did you do?

I answered _____ questions correctly.

Knowing You from A to Z

How well do you know your holiday guests? Use a **pencil** to write the letters A through Z (feel free to leave out the X!) on a piece of **paper**. Cut out each letter with **scissors,** and put all the letters into a **bowl.** Mix them up. Ask guests to sit in a circle. Players pass the bowl around and each chooses a letter. To start, the first player must tell something she knows about the person sitting on her right that others may not know, starting with the letter she picked. For example, if a player chooses the letter B, she might say, "Madeline loves banana bread." If she's wrong or can't think of anything about that person, she's out. The game continues until one person remains.

The Perceptive Pal award goes to _____

Dreidel Delight

To play this traditional Hanukkah game, you'll need a **dreidel** and **20 pennies per player.** For each round, every player puts 2 pennies in the "pot" in the center. The first player spins the dreidel. She makes a move depending on what letter the dreidel lands on when it stops spinning.

Use this key:

Nun: Do nothing.

Gimel: Take everything.

Hey: Take half of the pot.

Shin: Put 1 penny in the pot.

The winner is the one who wins all the coins from the other players.

The Super Spinner award goes to

_____

Boogie-Woogie

Sit or stand in a circle. Going around the circle, each girl says her name and creates a rhythm to go with her name. For example, the first player says, "My name is Alexa," and she claps 3 times. The next player says, "My name is Rachel," snaps her fingers, and then says, "Her name is Alexa," and repeats the 3 claps. This continues around the circle. Girls who forget names and rhythms are out. Who can repeat the most names and rhythms?

The Best Beat award goes to _____

Black Eyes

Use **paper** and a **pencil** to draw a ghost's outline. Place the ghost on the ground in front of you. Standing over the ghost with your arm out straight, drop a flat black button. Repeat with a second button. Now ask your opponent to drop her buttons. The one who keeps both eyes inside the outline wins. To break a tie, the winner is the one who places her eyes closest to the ghost's head.

The Eye Catcher award goes to

_____

Ghost Busters

This game works best at night. Ask a friend to hide cotton balls (ghosts) in plain view in a room. Don't tuck them behind things! Turn out the lights and grab a flashlight. You have 1 minute to find as many ghosts as you can. Now switch places and give your friend a chance.

My ghost score: _____

My partner's ghost score: _____

Creature Feature

Fold a piece of **paper** into thirds. Your friend does the same. At the top of the paper, draw a monster's head with a pencil, pen, or marker, making the neck go a little past the fold. Your friend does the same. Next, fold the paper so that your friend can't see the head, and trade papers. No peeking! Continue to draw the creature's waist and body a little past the fold, and switch papers again. Now draw the mystery creature's legs and feet. When you're done, unfold the papers to reveal your crazy creatures!

The Coolest Creature award goes to

Dancing Ghosts

With a black marker, draw eyes on white balloons and give one to each player. On "Boo!" each player taps her balloon to keep it in the air. Here's the catch: No one can move her feet once the game starts! If a balloon touches the ground, that player sits out. The one who can keep her "ghost" floating the longest wins.

Tougher: Two players entwine arms, using only one arm each to keep the ghost in the air.

The Galloping Ghost award goes to

Fashion Mummy

Divide into teams of 3. Give each team a roll of toilet paper. Each team wraps itself together in the paper, making one wide mummy. Once the teams are ready, on "Go!" see which team can walk the farthest without coming apart completely. **Tougher:** One team member closes her eyes as the other team members guide her progress.

The Model Mummy award goes to

Over and Under

Divide into 2 teams of at least 3 players per team. One team at a time competes. On "Go!" a player passes a roll of toilet paper over the next person's head, and that person passes the roll under the next person's legs, and so on, moving the paper up and down the line. While watching, the other teams count how many people the competing team wraps without breaking the paper. Then the next team competes. The team that goes over and under the most times wins.

The Relay Ruler award goes to

Monster Mosh

Turn on some music and have everyone dance.
When the music stops, everyone strikes a monster
pose—the scarier the better.

The Most Monstrous award goes to

_____

Challenge Yourself

Don't stop now! Give yourself challenges that will improve your confidence. If you love gymnastics, plan out small goals to master those skills one step at a time. If you struggle with reading, challenge yourself to finish a certain number of books in a set time. If you have a homework project, map out the steps, set mini deadlines, and then "Go!" Remember to celebrate your accomplishments with a homemade certificate or with a reward that you've promised yourself beforehand— such as a movie, a treat, or permission to spend an entire day with someone special.

Puzzle Answers

Name-Calling: 1. core + T + knee = Courtney; 2. bell + A = Bella; 3. tail + OR = Taylor; 4. bridge + IT = Bridget; 5. shell + bee = Shelby; 6. rocks + AN = Roxanne; 7. eye + lean = Eileen; 8. wand + A = Wanda.

Block Buster: 1. feeling blue; 2. double Dutch; 3. orange tree; 4. tickled pink; 5. goldfish; 6. three little pigs; 7. Jack-in-the-box; 8. blueberries; 9. double dare; 10. green thumb; 11. three strikes and you are out; 12. red in the face.

Zookeeper: 1. ape; 2. clam; 3. bat; 4. hare; 5. wasp; 6. deer; 7. cat; 8. wolf; 9. ant; 10. horse; 11. owl; 12. lamb; 13. eel; 14. newt; 15. dog; 16. seal; 17. rat; 18. gnu; 19. bear; 20. gnat.

Your challenge is to send us a letter telling us your favorite challenges or sharing with us even more challenges! Send your letters to:

Take the Challenge Editor
American Girl
8400 Fairway Place
Middleton, WI 53562

(All comments and suggestions received by American Girl may be used without compensation or acknowledgment. We're sorry, but we can't return photos.)

Here are some other American Girl books you might like:

❑ I read it.

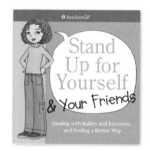

❑ I read it.

❑ I read it.

❑ I read it.

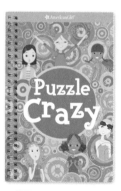

❑ I read it.

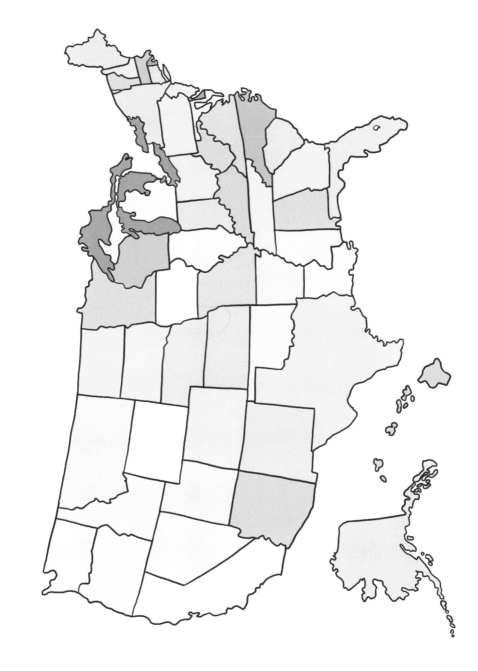

Penny Pincher

_____
(name)

Picnic Packer

_____
(name)

Marvelous Memory

_____
(name)

State Champion

_____
(name)

Haiku Know-How

_____
(name)

Mind Magician

_____
(name)

Book It

_____
(name)

Poetic Pluck

_____
(name)

Great Eights

_____
(name)

Zine Queen

_____
(name)

Top Hopper

_____
(name)

Tango Trotter

_____
(name)

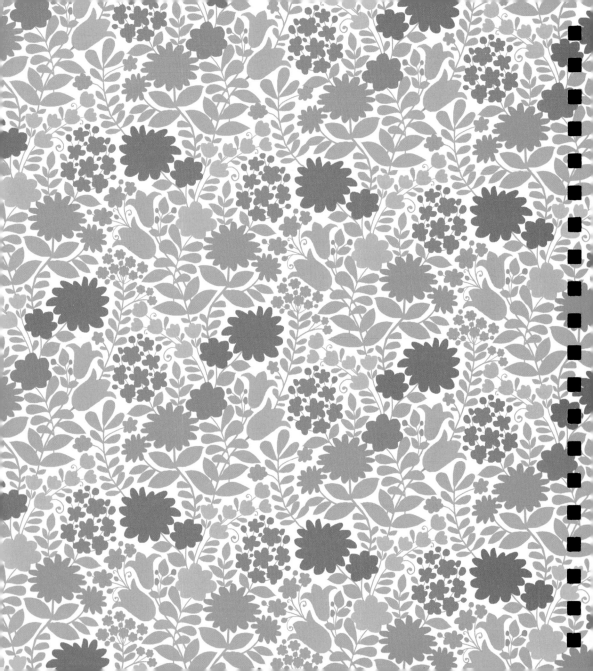

Golden Roller

_____
(name)

Terrific Tosser

_____
(name)

Soft Touch

_____
(name)

Pinsetter

_____
(name)

Platter Pride

_____
(name)

Double Trouble

_____
(name)

Bank Teller

_____
(name)

Size Wise

_____
(name)

Batches of Matches

_____
(name)

Puzzle Assembler

_____
(name)

Great Mate

_____
(name)

Smart Shopper

_____
(name)

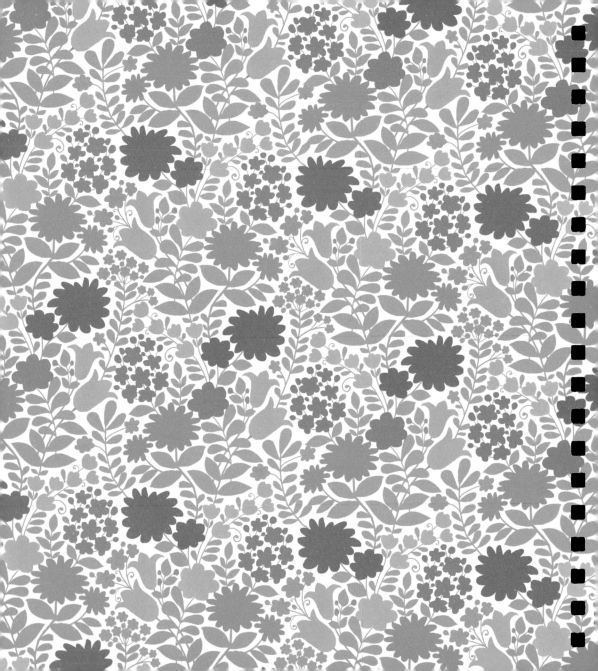

Card Sharp

_____
(name)

Lucky Duck

_____
(name)

Word Wizard

_____
(name)

Quick Change

_____
(name)

Rad Reporter

_____
(name)

Superstar

_____
(name)

Flower Power

_____
(name)

Silliest Storyteller

_____
(name)

Chatting Champion

_____
(name)

Champion Chicken

_____
(name)

Steadiest Spoon

_____
(name)

Triangular Ace

_____
(name)

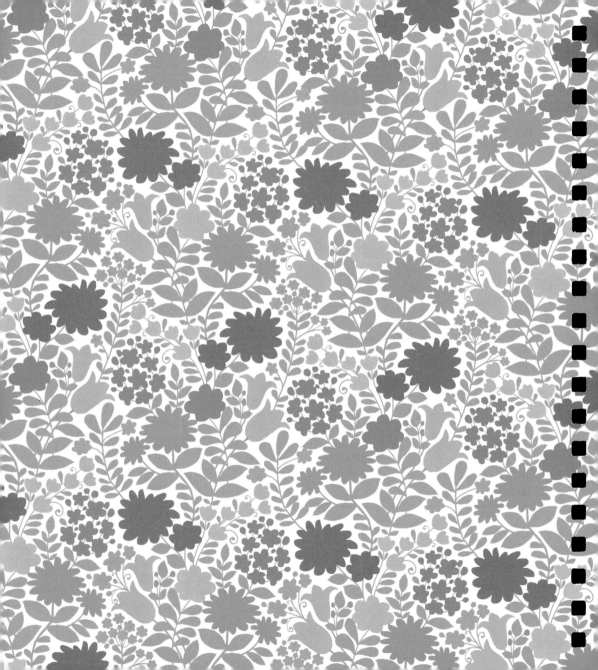

Tallest Tower

_____
(name)

Three-of-a-Kind

_____
(name)

Best Dressed

_____
(name)

Tiniest Island

_____
(name)

Strong and Silent

_____
(name)

Sweet Singer

_____
(name)

Ultimate Usability

_____
(name)

Frozen Foot

_____
(name)

Motor Mouth

_____
(name)

Head of Horseshoes

_____
(name)

Snow Shoveler

_____
(name)

Gift Grab

_____
(name)

Tom Turkey

_____
(name)

Super Spinner

_____
(name)

Galloping Ghost

_____
(name)

Delicious Dreamer

_____
(name)

Best Beat

_____
(name)

Model Mummy

_____
(name)

Stupendous Stumper

_____
(name)

Eye Catcher

_____
(name)

Relay Ruler

_____
(name)

Perceptive Pal

_____
(name)

Coolest Creature

_____
(name)

Most Monstrous

_____
(name)

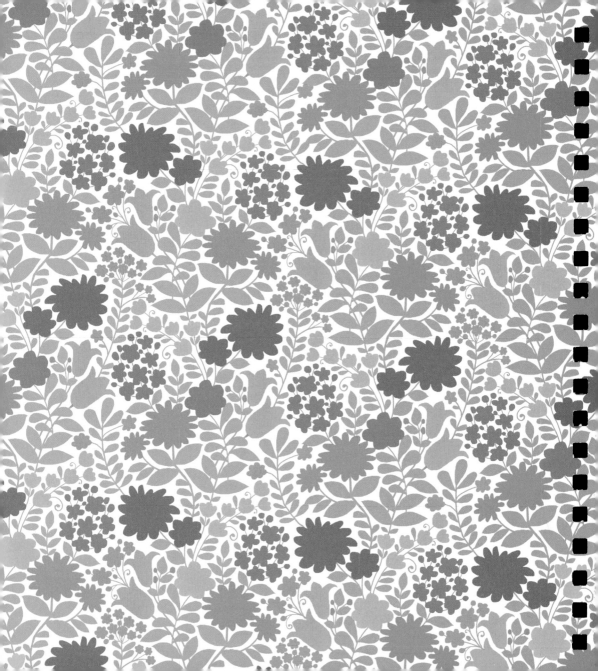

Try *American Girl* magazine!

SUPER Summer Issue! ☀ 4 Great Posters You'll Love

American Girl

35 ways to cool off and get **wet!**

☀ Make frozen **treats**

☀3 **quizzes** you can take

☀ Fun fruity **crafts**

Bonus! 4 funny bookmarks inside!

Simply mail this card today

Mail this card to receive a **risk-free** Preview Issue and start your one-year subscription. For just $22.95, you'll receive 6 bimonthly issues! If you don't love *American Girl®* right away, just write "cancel" on your invoice. The Preview Issue is yours to keep, free!

The magazine especially for girls 8 and up!

☐ 1 year (6 issues) $22.95

Send magazine to: *(please print)*

_____ / ___ / ___
Girl's name   Birth date *(optional)*

_____
Address

_____
City   State   Zip

Send bill to: *(please print)*

_____
Adult's name

_____
Address

_____
City   State   Zip

_____
Adult's signature

Guarantee: You may cancel at any time for a full refund on all unserved issues. Allow 4-6 weeks for first issue. Non-U.S. subscriptions are $29 U.S., prepaid only. To learn more about *American Girl* magazine or remove your name from our mailing list, please call 800-234-1278. Visit us online at americangirlmagazine.com. © 2011 American Girl, LLC.

K11AGL

Books are just the beginning...

Discover dolls, clothing, furniture, and accessories that inspire girls to imagine their own stories.

Request a FREE catalogue!

Just mail this card, call **800-845-0005,** or visit **americangirl.com.**

_____ / ___ / ___
Parent's name   Girl's birth date *(optional)*

_____
Address

_____
City   State   Zip

_____
Parent's e-mail *(For order information, updates, and Web-exclusive offers.)*

(_____)
Phone   ❏ Home ❏ Work

_____
Parent's signature   12583i

Send a catalogue to a grandparent or friend:

_____
Name

_____
Address

_____
City   State   Zip
                                            12591i

Today's date _____ / ___ / ___

BUSINESS REPLY MAIL

FIRST-CLASS MAIL   PERMIT NO. 190   BOONE IA

POSTAGE WILL BE PAID BY ADDRESSEE

NO POSTAGE
NECESSARY
IF MAILED
IN THE
UNITED STATES

★ American Girl®

Magazine Subscription Dept
PO BOX 5532
HARLAN IA 51593-3032

Welcome to
Fun for Girls!
Your online
place to play!

Visit americangirl.com
and click on **Fun for Girls**
for quizzes and games.

Place
Stamp
Here

★ American Girl®

PO BOX 620497
MIDDLETON WI 53562-0497